GROSS AND DISGUSTING ANIMALS

A Crabtree Branches Book

Julie K. Lundgren

CRABTREE
Publishing Company
www.crabtreebooks.com

School-to-Home Support for Caregivers and Teachers

This high-interest book is designed to motivate striving students with engaging topics while building fluency, vocabulary, and an interest in reading. Here are a few questions and activities to help the reader build upon his or her comprehension skills.

Before Reading:

- *What do I think this book is about?*
- *What do I know about this topic?*
- *What do I want to learn about this topic?*
- *Why am I reading this book?*

During Reading:

- *I wonder why...*
- *I'm curious to know...*
- *How is this like something I already know?*
- *What have I learned so far?*

After Reading:

- *What was the author trying to teach me?*
- *What are some details?*
- *How did the photographs and captions help me understand more?*
- *Read the book again and look for the vocabulary words.*
- *What questions do I still have?*

Extension Activities:

- *What was your favorite part of the book? Write a paragraph on it.*
- *Draw a picture of your favorite thing you learned from the book.*

TABLE OF CONTENTS

DON'T LOOK AWAY

Feeling brave? Discover creatures so gross, disgusting, and amazing, you can't look away. Check out animals with weapons of destruction and death, disgusting defenses, and offspring only a mother could love.

Sea lampreys attach to other fish and slowly kill them over several months.

Sea lampreys are like vacuums with teeth. They bite and suck blood and juices from victims.

EEW!
Epic Extreme Weirdness (EEW) exists everywhere!

The bird-dung crab spider has a wet look, like a fresh load of poop...

...or a dry look, like it's been there a while.

giant swallowtail caterpillar

Predators pass by animals that look like poop. Crud **camouflage** helps poop imposters ambush their prey, too.

bird poop frog

HORROR SHOW

Disturbing creatures live underwater, underground, and in extreme environments of all kinds. With their fantastically disgusting looks, they could star in monster movies!

Algae form a living hairstyle atop the Mary River turtle.

Decorating with the Dead

After eating its insect prey, a junk bug adds the leftover **corpses** to the pile on its back.

Speaking of stars, what if you had a nose shaped like a star? The star-nosed mole basically has a hand with 22 fingers attached to its face.

Star-nosed moles tunnel underground, searching for prey by touch and smell in the dark.

In the Dark
Cave centipedes creep and crawl under cover of darkness.

Meet some masters of slime.
Sea hares eat **algae** to make
toxic slime.

Sea hares squirt clouds of purple dye to escape predators.

Parrotfish sleep inside a bubble of their own snot.

Oozy Greatness

Hagfish make buckets of ooze. In 2017, a semi-truck full of live hagfish crashed, coating the road and cars with thick slime and slithering fish.

DISGUSTING DINING

Which animal is a Monster Chef? Camel spiders chop and slice flesh, flood it with digestive juices, then slurp up the soup.

Camel spiders, or wind scorpions, use their huge, powerful jaws to saw up prey.

Camel spiders eat insects, rodents, and lizards, not people.

Craving a warm meal? Cave roaches love to feast on a pile of fresh bat **guano.** If a bat corpse happens to fall in, that only makes it better.

Scavengers like cave roaches clean up leftovers.

EEW!
Imagine spreading your poop around to attract beetles to eat, like the burrowing owl does. Yum?

Freaky weapons help animals capture dinner. The aye-aye taps trees with its long middle finger, listening for grubs inside. It uses that same finger to reach deep into the tree to hook and pull out the grub. Knock, knock, creepy crawly!

Aye-ayes are lemurs with fingers like fishing poles.

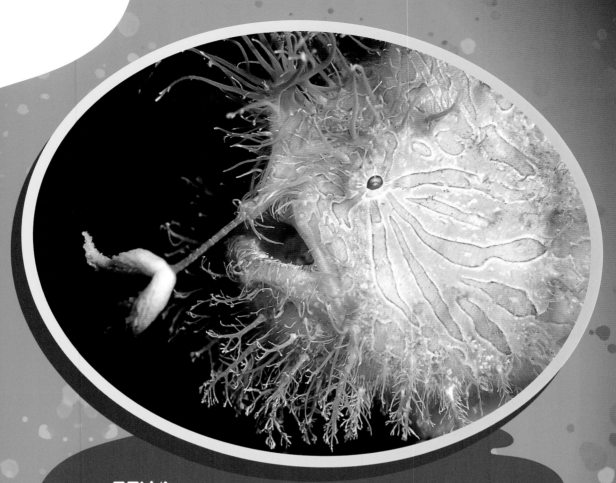

EEW!
To lure prey, the hairy frogfish has a body part sticking out from its forehead that looks like a wiggling, tasty worm.

BLOOD, GUTS, AND A GHASTLY STINK

Animal defenses can be insanely gross! Sea cucumbers fart their guts out their butts to scare away predators. Later, they grow new parts.

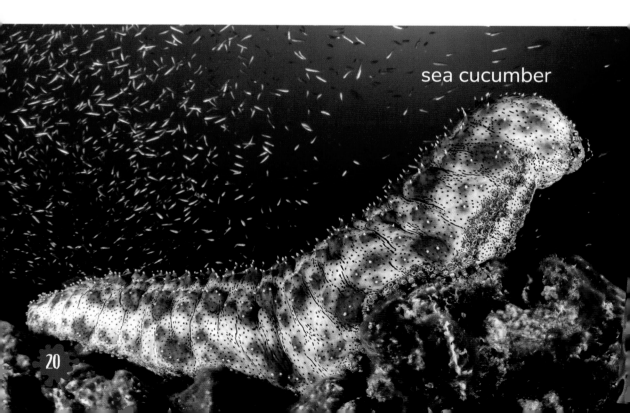

sea cucumber

To escape predators, some horned lizards spurt streams of blood from their eyes.

Some sea cucumbers bomb pesky predators with special sticky organs. The sea cucumbers make more in 2 to 3 weeks.

Who is the ultimate butt bomber? The **bombardier** beetle's spray smells and tastes so bad, a toad that eats one will pop its stomach inside out to dump out the beetle.

Bombardier beetles rotate their rears to aim and fire off a spray of acid.

SPLAT!

Fulmar chicks spew stinky, harmful fish smoothies at enemies.

23

Other animals defend by stench, too. **Opossums** poop super smelly green **mucus.** Giant African millipedes make a strong spray that comes out of each segment of their bodies. Clear the room!

The toxic and stinky spray from giant African millipedes can kill a mouse!

opossum

GRUESOME OFFSPRING

Ready for more? More is where we're headed next with disgusting animal offspring. Burying beetles lay their eggs in dead mice. The mother beetle eats the mouse, then pukes to feed the hatched **larvae.**

If there isn't enough food to go around, the burying beetle will eat her own larvae.

Major EEW!
The Surinam toad is
the original hatchback. The mother
toad carries her eggs on her back and
they hatch out of her skin.

Of course, poop features in this horror story. Blue bottle flies lay their eggs in dung, corpses, and garbage. The larvae eat their stinky but still nutritious homes.

Scientists use the stage of larvae development to help determine how long a decaying body has been dead.

What do you think of all this EEW? Animals may be gross and disgusting, but still awesome!

Plot Twist!
Epomis beetle larvae look tasty to frogs. However, they latch onto the frog's tongue and inject a toxin that **paralyzes** and digests the frog.

GLOSSARY

algae (AL-jee): Aquatic plants that use sunlight to grow and are eaten by many animals

bombardier (bom-bar-DEER): An expert at aiming and launching bombs

camouflage (KAM-uh-flahzh): Colorations that help animals blend in or pretend to be something else

corpses (KORP-sihz): Dead bodies

guano (GWAH-no): Bat droppings, or poop

larvae (LAR-vee): In insects, the stage of development between egg and adult

mucus (MEW-kuss): Slimy substance produced by animals and humans

opossums (uh-PAH-sumz): Furry nocturnal animals about the size of a cat

paralyzes (PAIR-uh-lye-zihz): Causes an inability to move

toxic (TAHK-sick): Harmful, with the ability to sicken or kill

INDEX

WEBSITES TO VISIT

https://animals.net/nature-is-gross-four-disgusting-habits-of-four-interesting-animals/

https://onekindplanet.org/top-10/top-10-worlds-smelliest-animals/

https://zoo.sandiegozoo.org/animals-plants

ABOUT THE AUTHOR
Julie K. Lundgren

Julie K. Lundgren grew up on the north shore of Lake Superior, a place of woods, water, and adventure. She loves bees, dragonflies, old trees, and science and has a special place in her heart for disgustingly cool animals. Her interests led her to a degree in biology and a lifelong curiosity about wild places.

CRABTREE
Publishing Company

Produced by: Blue Door Education
for Crabtree Publishing
Written by: Julie K. Lundgren
Designed by: Jennifer Dydyk
Edited by: Tracy Nelson Maurer
Proofreader: Crystal Sikkens

Photographs: Cover photo © Laura Dts, cover splat art on cover and throughout © SpicyTruffel, page 4 © Nicolas Primola, page 5 (top) © Gena Melendrez, (bottom) © Olga_Serova, page 6 (top) © Pong Wira, (bottom) © Alen thien, page 7 (top) © Brian Magnier, (bottom) © Rosa Jay, page 8 © Rob D the Baker, page 9 © SIMON SHIM, page 10 (top) © VetraKori, (bottom) © Agnieszka Bacal, page 11 © CPbackpacker, page 12 (top) © scubaluna, page 13 (bottom) © Liliya Butenko, page 14 and page 15 (top) © Dr.MYM, page 15 (bottom) © Ondrej Michalek, page 16 © Ianaid12, page 17 (top) © Maximillian cabinet, (bottom) © Don Mammoser, page 18 © Dan Tiego, page 19 © Jack PhotoWarp, page 20 © Richard Whitcombe, page 21 (top) © Milan Zygmunt, illustration © Sergey Mikhaylov, (bottom photo) © Ethan Daniels, page 22 photo © THE PICTURE RESEARCHER, slime illustration © Arcady, page 23 (top) photo © By KASIRA SUDA, illustration inside inset © Blue Door Education, SPLAT illustration © ByeByeSSTK, (bottom) photo © Nick Pecker, page 24 photo © Wandel Guides, illustration © ianlusung, page 25 © Lisa Hagan, opossum illustration © Bistraffic, poop illustration © Arcady, page 26 © Tobyphotos, page 27 (top) © Dan Olsen, (bottom) © Jason Patrick Ross, page 28 (top) © Avaniks, (center) © Be Shearer, (bottom) © Ton Bangkeaw. All images from Shutterstock.com except page12 parrotfish © Igor Cristino Silva Cruz (Wikipedia) https://creativecommons.org/licenses/by-sa/4.0/deed.en, page 13 Scientists photo courtesy of NOAA, page 29 © Wizen G, Gasith A https://creativecommons.org/licenses/by/3.0/deed.en

Library and Archives Canada Cataloguing in Publication

Title: Gross and disgusting animals / Julie K. Lundgren.
Names: Lundgren, Julie K., author.
Description: Series statement: Gross and disgusting things | "A Crabtree branches book" | Includes index.
Identifiers: Canadiana (print) 20210220449 | Canadiana (ebook) 20210220457 | ISBN 9781427154460 (hardcover) | ISBN 9781427154521 (softcover) | ISBN 9781427154583 (HTML) | ISBN 9781427154644 (EPUB) | ISBN 9781427154705 (read-along ebook)
Subjects: LCSH: Animals—Juvenile literature. | LCSH: Animals—Miscellanea—Juvenile literature. | LCSH: Zoology—Juvenile literature. | LCSH: Zoology—Miscellanea—Juvenile literature.
Classification: LCC QL49 .L86 2022 | DDC j590—dc23

Library of Congress Cataloging-in-Publication Data

Names: Lundgren, Julie K., author.
Title: Gross and disgusting animals / Julie K. Lundgren.
Description: New York : Crabtree Publishing, 2022. | Series: Gross and disgusting things - a Crabtree branches book | Includes index.
Identifiers: LCCN 2021022354 (print) | LCCN 2021022355 (ebook) | ISBN 9781427154460 (hardcover) | ISBN 9781427154521 (paperback) | ISBN 9781427154583 (ebook) | ISBN 9781427154644 (epub) | ISBN 9781427154705
Subjects: LCSH: Predatory animals--Juvenile literature. | Animal behavior--Juvenile literature.
Classification: LCC QL758 .L86 2022 (print) | LCC QL758 (ebook) | DDC 591.5/3--dc23
LC record available at https://lccn.loc.gov/2021022354
LC ebook record available at https://lccn.loc.gov/2021022355

Crabtree Publishing Company

www.crabtreebooks.com   1-800-387-7650

Copyright © 2022 **CRABTREE PUBLISHING COMPANY**   Printed in the U.S.A./072021/CG20210514

Published in the United States
Crabtree Publishing
347 Fifth Avenue, Suite 1402-145
New York, NY, 10016

Published in Canada
Crabtree Publishing
616 Welland Ave.
St. Catharines, ON, L2M 5V6